The Bobwhite Quail

by W.S. Taylor

with an introduction by Jackson Chambers

Self Reliance Books

Get more historic titles on animal and stock breeding, gardening and old fashioned skills by visiting us at:

http://selfreliancebooks.blogspot.com/

Introduction

I am pleased to present yet another title on Raising Quail.

This volume is entitled "Quailology" and was published by Fred Kerr in 1903.

The work is in the Public Domain and is re-printed here in accordance with Federal Laws.

As with all reprinted books of this age that are intended to perfectly reproduce the original edition, considerable pains and effort had to be undertaken to correct fading and sometimes outright damage to existing proofs of this title. At times, this task is quite monumental, requiring an almost total "rebuilding" of some pages from digital proofs of multiple copies. Despite this, imperfections still sometimes exist in the final proof and may detract from the visual appearance of the text.

I hope you enjoy reading this book as much as I enjoyed making it available to readers again.

Jackson Chambers

Kellerstrass Farm
Arthur Oscar Schilling
1907

FOREWORD.

Texas was once bountifully blessed with wild life. It was the hunter's paradise. Less than half a century ago, hunters came from afar to hunt big game in Texas, for at that time great herds of buffalo roamed over our western plains.

Just a few years ago antelope hunting and pairie-hen shooting were all that the sportsman and hunter could desire. Today our antelope are all but exterminated, and the prairie hen is very, very rare in the State. Turkey and deer, once abundant in Texas, are gradually going the way of the antelope and the prairie hen.

The wild turkey cannot hold its own against all its natural enemies and the long open season. The limit of three birds a season is not adhered to, and the close of each open season sees our largest game bird so greatly reduced in numbers that it is evident it is facing rapid extinction under present conditions.

While the outlook for deer is somewhat brighter, their numbers are decreasing in Texas annually, and each year sees them crowded into a smaller area in the State. The open season and the three-buck limit, if reduced, would help to preserve their numbers and insure good hunting. If the deer are properly protected, we shall have an abundance of them in Texas for all time. Unless better protection is afforded them, we shall have no deer hunting in less than half a century.

There are fewer quail in Texas today than ever before. The excessive drought that has prevailed over large areas of central, south and west Texas has made it difficult for the birds to propagate. Very few birds have been reared in the drought area for the past two seasons. Hunters have not been slow, however, to kill off the breeding stock. Many men who drive through the country in a car carry a gun and take a "pot shot" at every covey they see. This is a most unsportsmanlike thing. It is as bad as trapping or netting the birds. We need a stronger sentiment for the protection, preservation and propagation of this wonderful little game bird. The purpose of this little bulletin is to interest the boys and girls of Texas in the protection and preservation of the bobwhite, and thereby interest them in the protection and preservation of the blue quail, Mearn's quail, and all other forms of wild life in Texas.

Our fathers hunted buffalo, antelope and sage grouse. We are hunting deer, turkey and quail. What kind of heritage of wild life will the next generation receive from our hands? If we are as wasteful as our fathers were, our children will hunt rabbits, as the children in many of the States where game once abounded are compelled to do today. With the automobile and pumpgun, our hunters are far more effective than were the hunters in our father's day. Our heritage of game and wild life is one of the greatest assets of our state. Let us protect and preserve it for the generations that are to come.

I desire to express my high appreciation of the articles that follow by Dr. Forbush and Major Shufeldt.

WILLIAM SEPTIMUS TAYLOR.

THE QUAIL

(Written especially for this bulletin by Dr. E. H. Forbush,
State Ornithologist of Massachusetts.)

There is no bird that contributes more to man's comfort and welfare and to the joy of living than Bob-white. His call is heartening, it carries the irrepressible gladness of the spring. It is the very expression of good cheer. No bird is more destructive to weeds and insect pests that plague the farmer and gardener and add to the high cost of living for us all. Our little friend feeds largely on the seeds of weeds and on pernicious insects. Here are sample insect meals eaten by a single bird: 12 squash bugs, 39 grasshoppers, 100 chinch bugs, 568 mosquitos, and 2,326 plant lice. Each one of these numbers represents the insects eaten by a single bird at one meal. Large insects were eaten as follows: 101 potato beetles, 8 white grubs, 12 army worms, 12 cutworms. One Bob-white ate 1,350 flies in a day, another 1,289 rose slugs, another 700 miscellaneous insects, of which 300 were grasshoppers. In some parts of the country farmers lease the shooting privileges on their land to people who hunt this bird, and the farmers receive in return more than the taxes on the land. Thus indirectly Bob-white pays for the education of the children. Large sums of money are spent over a great part of the United States by sportsmen in the pursuit of this little bird, and a great business is carried on in sportsmen's supplies with Bob-white as the object. But considering the usefulness of this small game bird to the farm, many farmers believe that it should be protected from shooting at all times, and some states now give it such protection.

Boston, February 1, 1918.   E. H. FORBUSH,
                              State Ornithologist of Massachusetts.

A PLEA FOR THE PRESERVATION OF THE BOB-WHITE IN TEXAS.

(Written especially for this bulletin by Major R. W. Shufeldt, of the U. S. A. Medical Corps, one of the most distinguished American ornithologists.)

Notwithstanding the commendable efforts of the game-law makers; the endeavors of the various private and national bird-protection societies, and the warnings of prominent ornithologists, the game-birds, especially those of the gallinaceous group, are being slowly but very surely exterminated all over the United States. Now, during the past ten years an enormous body of literature has appeared on the value of the insectivorous birds of the country to the farmer and agriculturists generally, while comparatively little has been said, one way or the other, in regard to the part that quails play in this matter.

Right here I desire to say but a very few words on this subject; but these I have weighed well, as an observing ornithologist of half a century's experience. I can say that we have no bird among all those species that devour harmful insects, that is a greater friend of the farmer than the Texan Bob-white. Every bird in nature of that species is worth ten times its weight in gold each year or season that passes on account of the enormous number of insects it destroys, the latter being of a class that falls distinctly into the category of those that are inimical to the success of the farmer's crops and grain.

Man destroys more Bob-whites in a year—that is, the gunners of the state do—than any other agent known to me, including the mammals and birds of prey. The Bob-whites should be rigidly protected by law for several years to come, especially against guns, traps, and other means leading to their extermination. Faithfully yours,

F. W. SHUFELDT.

Washington, D. C., January 24, 1918.

Courtesy National Association of Audubon Societies

BOB WHITE

He is truly the king of his race, and not only that, for, in the opinion of hosts of enthusiastic sportsmen, he is the best bird that flies.—Edwyn Sandys.

THE BOBWHITE

Distribution

The bobwhite is by far the most common quail in the United States. It is our most popular game bird, and is distributed over a large area. The statement is often heard that "rain follows the plow." If some one had said that the "bobwhite follows the plow," he would have been approximating the truth. It is distinctly a bird of civilized communities. While it cannot stand extreme cold without shelter, it ranges widely, and is able to hold its own as far north as southern Canada. The bobwhite is found all over the eastern half of the United States and west to the Rockies.

Description

The bobwhite does not need to be described to the people of Texas, nor do the people of any other state east of the Rockies. It is more widely known, perhaps, than any bird of the United States, save the mourning dove. It is known in the Southern States as partridge; in the North, it is commonly known as quail, and everywhere it is known as bobwhite. Although not a bird of rare beauty, its "trim, alert figure and its tasteful color pattern of black, white and brown, set off with delicate tintings of blue-gray," cannot help but command admiration. The fearlessness and daring of the bird as it runs in the road ahead of the traveler, or as it flies just a few inches from the nose of the dog, are traits which win admiration for it everywhere. The bobwhite is commonly supposed to have a crest. The crest is a characteristic of most American quails, but in the bobwhite it is invisible, except when the bird is excited.

Our Texas bobwhite differs slightly in color from its northern and eastern relatives. It is paler, and has a rufous collar.

Call Notes

When the covey begins to break up into pairs in the spring, the nuptial call of the male bird is an unmistakable guide to his identity. He perches himself on a log or stump, and then comes that clear, mellow call, so characteristic of early spring and summer. "The plowman hears it as he drives his team afield, and it mingles with the ringing sound of the whetstone on the scythe." To the sportsman, the familiar challenge sounds like "bobwhite" or "bob-bobwhite," while the farmer frequently interprets it as "more-wet" or "some-more-wet." The note is a beautiful, clear whistle, and may be heard quite a distance. The bird can reduce the volume of the note, and does so at the approach of danger, so that frequently one thinks he is quite a distance from the source of the call when in reality he is very near it.

There is no forgetting the wistful, plaintive note of the quail that is used to reassemble the flock after it has been scattered by the gunner. A bird will call out "ka-loi-kee, ka-loi-kee," and another bird will answer "whoil-kee." These notes are used by both the male and female birds, the first note being the rallying call and the latter the answering cry. What man in the country has not heard the low, tender call of the mother quail to her young, "ka-loi-kee, ka-loi-kee"? What sportsman has not felt his pulse quicken in the late afternoon at hearing the same note from a lone bird scattered from the flock and then hearing the clear, vibrant answer, "whoil-kee" come from almost under his feet? There is a tenderness and longing expressed in these two notes, when uttered by lone birds of a scattered flock, that once heard cannot be forgotten.

Roosting Habits

Mr. Forbush, in *Useful Birds and Their Protection*, describes the roosting habits of the bobwhite as follows: "At night they sleep on the ground in a ring, heads out and shoulder to shoulder. In this formation there are always some birds to face and discover danger, upon whichever side it approaches. One spring into the air gives each bird wing, and off they fly in all directions, an animated 'feather bombshell,' exploding in the darkness with a roar of pinions sufficient to startle and possibly baffle an enemy."

The birds seem to prefer the open fields for roosting places, but the writer has found them roosting in large coveys in dense thickets or in woodlands. They probably roost under cover more during the hunting season, due to the fact that they are frequently disturbed and driven to cover in the late afternoon by hunters.

Nests and Nesting

The nest of the bobwhite is built on the ground. It is usually to be found in meadows, green fields, or along fence rows and roadsides grown up with grass, weeds and brush. The nest is built of grass, and is arched over so completely that it seems to be built at the end of a tunnel. The arch provides rather a safe hiding place for the ten to sixteen white eggs usually found in the bobwhite's nest. Occasionally a nest is found with as many as twenty-four eggs, and one instance is on record, I believe, where forty-two eggs were found in one nest. In all probability more than one bird was using the nest in the latter case, and may have been in the former.

The time of nesting is variable. May and June are the main months for nesting in Texas, but there are records in numbers for June and July and August. September and April also come in for records.

The number of nestings a season by a single pair is an undecided question. We know that if a nest is destroyed the birds usually go to work immediately to build another. The records of late nestings and the fact that birds of two sizes are sometimes found with the mother bird would seem to indicate that the bobwhite rears two broods a season at times, but definite information on the subject is lacking. Some authorities think that, in rare instances, the birds rear three broods a season. Here again definite information is lacking.

Young Quail

Baby quail are said to leave the nest the moment they are hatched. This probably is somewhat exaggerated, but it is very likely that all the eggs hatch about the same time and the baby chicks leave the nest very soon thereafter. The newly hatched young are very small, downy, brown-streaked and resemble bantam or brown leghorn chicks. These tiny babies tuck themselves

Photographed by Elton Perry, Austin, Texas

NEST AND EGGS OF BOB-WHITE

Note the sharply pointed eggs. In natural position eggs are closely packed in nest with points downward.

close to the earth, and close their eyes at the first danger signal from the mother. Their protective coloring renders them practically invisible when squatting motionless. It is well to stand still several minutes after disturbing the young to give the mother bird time to call them away; otherwise there is a chance that the baby birds will be stepped on.

Mr. Nash, in discussing the food of young quail, says that they eat their own weight in insects daily. It is difficult to estimate the good a pair of birds with a flock of baby bobwhites will do on a farm. Young birds are always hungry, and their food is made up almost wholly of insect enemies of the farm and garden. There ought to be a pair of birds with a brood of chicks for every two acres of cultivated land in Texas.

The Broken-Wing Stunt of the Quail

Few people living in the country where the quail breeds have failed to observe the simulation of a broken wing by birds desiring to decoy men and dogs away from their nests. This characteristic is not common to the quail alone by any means. Many birds practice it. Doves frequently fall off their nests and appear to be able to fly only with the most intense pain and by the greatest effort. A mother quail, when scared from her nest, or when an enemy approaches her brood, will frequently tumble over on her side and flutter along on the ground just in front of the boy or dog, until the enemy is drawn a considerable distance from the nest. Sometimes the bird, when pursued by a dog, in her eagerness to get the enemy a great distance from the nest or from her babies, stays just a foot or so in front of the dog's nose. Occasionally she takes too big a chance and is caught.

Food Habits of the Bobwhite

A great many careful studies of the food of the bobwhite have been made. Perhaps the most interesting and most scientific of these are the experiments made by the biological survey at Washington and the simple but accurate experiments of Dr. Clifton F. Hodge and Mrs. Margaret Morse Nice.

The biological survey sums up, in Farmers' Bulletin No. 755, the results of many years of study and investigation, as follows: "Weed seeds form more than half of the total food,

SCALED PARTRIDGE

and include those of all the worst weed pests of the farm. Among them may be mentioned crab grass, cockspur, witch and foxtail grasses, sheep sorrel, smart weed, bindweed, lamb's quarters, pigweed, corn cockle, chickweed, chalock, partridge pea, beggar lice, nail grass, rib grass, ragweed and Spanish needles.

"Acorn, beechnuts, chestnuts and pine seeds make up about 2.5 per cent of the food, and wild fruits about 10 per cent. The fruits include berries of palmetto, smilax, wax myrtle, mulberry, sassafras, blackberry, raspberries, rose haws, cherry, sumac, grapes, sour gum, blueberries, honeysuckle, partridge berry and a number of others. The bobwhite feeds to a slight extent upon buds and leaves, including those of yellow and red sorrel, cinquefoil and clover.

"Grain forms scarcely more than a sixth of the food, but most of it is taken during winter and early spring, when nothing but waste grain is available. The habit of gleaning this after harvest is beneficial to the farm, for volunteer grain is not desirable, especially where it serves to maintain certain insects and fungus pests. Although most of the grain and seed crops grown upon the farm are represented in bobwhite's dietary, no significant damage can be attributed to the bird.

"Animal food, chiefly insects, composes nearly a sixth of the bird's subsistence. From June to August, inclusive, when insects are most numerous, their proportion in the food is about 36 per cent. The variety of insect food is great, and includes a number of the most destructive agricultural pests. Among them may be mentioned the Colorado potato beetle, twelve-spotted cucumber beetle, bean leaf beetle, squash ladybird, wireworms, May beetles, corn pillbugs, clover leaf weevil, cotton boll weevil, army worm, bollworm, cutworms and chinch bug."

The data above are the results of the examination of many stomachs of birds taken all over the United States. The data as given by Dr. Hodge and Mrs. Nice were obtained from feeding quail in captivity.*

---

*The data as given from the work of Dr. Hodge and Mrs. Nice have been taken almost verbatim from *Game Birds, Wild Fowl and Shore; Birds,* by Edward H. Forbush.

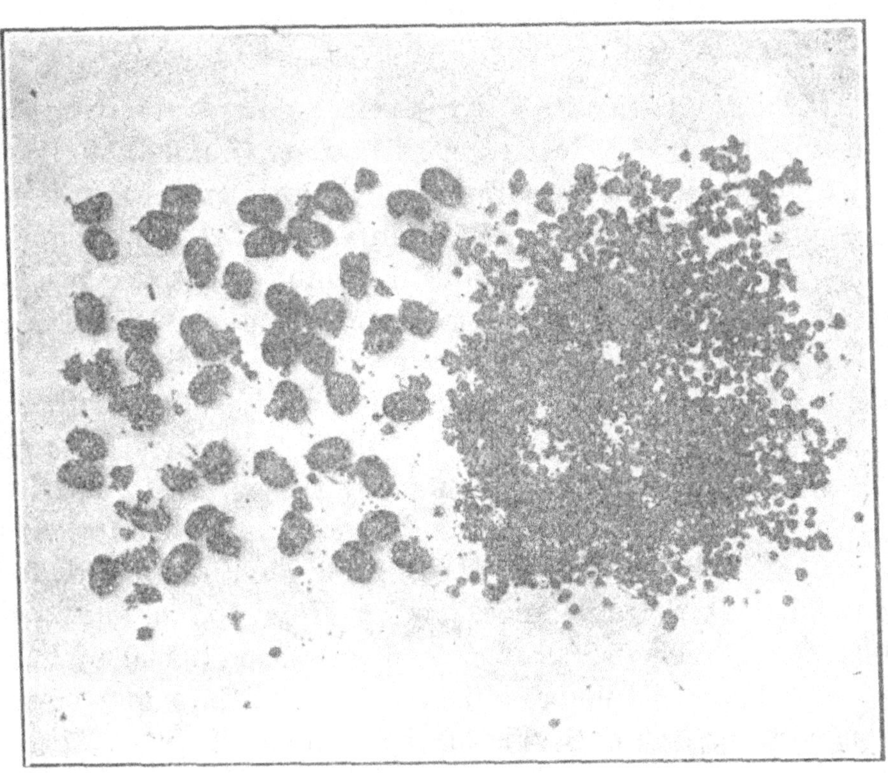

CONTENTS OF A QUAIL'S STOMACH

Courtesy of Dr. E. H. Farbush
State Ornithologist of Massachusetts

A COVEY OF QUAIL

Dr. Hodge and Mrs. Nice have given us some interesting facts concerning the food habits of quail. Each number of insects given represents the largest number eaten during a single meal by one bird. Chinch bugs, 100; plant lice, 2,326; grasshoppers, 39; mosquitoes, 568; potato beetles, 101, etc. Mrs. Nice also kept a record of the number of insects eaten by a single bird in one day. In the following, each number given represents the number of insects eaten by one bird in one day: Chrysanthemum black flies, 5,000; flies, 1,350; rose slugs, 1,286. Mrs. Nice gives a list of 141 species of insects eaten by the bobwhite, nearly all of which are injurious, and a list of 129 weeds whose seeds the bird eats, all of which are injurious. The number of seeds taken by one bird at a single meal varies from 105 of stink-weed or 400 of pig-weed, 5,000 of pigeon grass, or 10,000 of lamb's quarters, while the number taken by one bird in a day varies from 600 of burdock to 30,000 of rabbit food clover.

There is a mistaken idea abroad that the bobwhite feeds heavily on the cotton boll weevil, and campaigns for the bird's protection have been waged frequently, using this as a slogan. The results up to this time do not show that the bobwhite feeds to any appreciable extent on the boll weevil. Reports from various sections that these birds are eating the boll weevil in large numbers are based on field observations, and are frequently inaccurate.

Fortunately, the bobwhite does not need this added characteristic to make it valuable. Its tremendous propensity for consuming other harmful insects and the seeds of various weeds makes it a most valuable friend and ally of the farm and the farmer.

There is still another erroneous impression regarding the bobwhite in the minds of some farmers. It is sometimes claimed that seed-eating birds fail to digest the seeds eaten and that the seeds of weeds are scattered by doves and quails especially. This is not true. The following statement from Dr. H. P. Attwater of Houston, is very clear on this point, and is corroborated by the biological institutions of the United States: "*Seeds consumed by doves, quail, finches and other seed-eating birds are eaten for the kernel they contain, and the grinding and digestion of this food necessarily destroys the seeds. Many fruits and berries, eaten by mocking-birds, thrushes and other species of birds are eaten solely for the nourishing matter or pulp which is attached to or surrounds the seed. In this case the seed often escapes destruction, and is discarded either by ejection or rejection, and by this means becomes scattered in that locality. In other words, seeds which are contained in nourishment are eaten and survive, while seeds which simply contain nourishment are eaten and destroyed."*

Present Abundance

That quail are on the decrease in Texas is an undisputed fact. A few years ago blue quail, Mearn's quail (fool quail) and bobwhite were abundant in their respective homes in Texas. Gradually the blue quail is being forced into a smaller territory of southwest Texas, and its numbers are becoming fewer every year. The Mearn's quail is all but extinct in Texas. Its gentle, unsuspicious disposition has proved fatal to its existence in the same way that the timid, trusting nature of the dove has done. The bobwhite, once abundant in practically all cultivated regions of Texas, is now very rare in many black-land counties, and is abundant in but few sections. That we have a good number of quail left is true. Many people would say we have an abundance of quail. But we do not have as many quail as we need, nor half as many as we should have.

Every farm in Texas should have one, two, three, or more coveys of bobwhites. There should be a bobwhite for every acre of cultivated land in Texas. Texas would have fewer weeds, would suffer smaller losses from depredations of injurious insects, and would reap more abundant harvests if she would preserve and propagate her quail. If a ranch will run a cow to every ten acres, no intelligent ranchman will stock it with only one cow to forty acres. If a farm will not only raise a bobwhite, one to every acre, but will raise greater crops as a result of raising a bobwhite on every acre, why not use our common sense and raise more bobwhites?

Game Laws and Protection

Many States have recognized the worth of the quail to the farmer and the gardener, and have stopped the killing of the bobwhite entirely for a period of years. There is no open season for shooting bobwhite in Arizona, California, Colorado, Iowa, Idaho, Kansas, Michigan, New Mexico, New York, Nevada, Ohio, North Dakota, South Dakota, Utah, Wisconsin and Wyoming, according to Mr. William F. Hornaday. A large group of States have open seasons for a few weeks each year, and many States have bag limits.

Texas has both an open season and a bag limit, neither of which is properly enforced. In the first place, we have never been able to develop in Texas a proper respect for game laws. The prairie hen has been practically exterminated during a long closed season. Our antelope have been slaughtered during a closed season, until we have just a very few left in the State. The protection offered our quail is but little better. A closed season in Texas does not insure protection. *Texas needs and should have a hunter's license for every individual who goes into the field to shoot game. In addition to this, Texas needs and should have a bird and game commissioner, with a system of wardens and deputy wardens over the State whose business it would be to see to it that the laws protecting the wild life of the State are rigidly enforced.* Secondly, our open season is too long. If we are even to maintain our number of quail, we must cut the season to one month. If we want to increase our quail supply—and surely we need to increase it—we should cut the season to two weeks. An open season for hunting quail from December 15 to January 1, with a bag limit of fifteen birds for one day, would, if properly enforced, insure an abundance of quail in Texas for all time.

The bobwhite is a game bird, and, in the writer's opinion, is the "best bird that flies." It is the constant friend and ally of the farmer. It works untiringly during the long hot summer months to protect the growing crops, and then toils unceasingly during the winter months destroying prospective weeds. Its labor never ends. Few farmers recognize its genuine worth, or its protection would be a matter of greater concern to them.

Courtesy of Dr. William T. Hornaday

THE MODERN JUGGERNAUT OF GAME SLAUGHTER

It was the automobile that made possible this deadly work by three men, pump guns and dog. Everything goes down before this combination. Under such conditions, how can we expect to preserve our wild game in Texas?

The sportsman and the farmer should join hands, not only in protecting and preserving the bird, but in perceptibly increasing its numbers in Texas.

What Others Say

He is the gleaner who never reaps, who guards the growing crops, who glories over a bounteous yield, yet is content to wait and watch for those lost grains which fall to him by right.—Edwyn Sandys.

A careful study of the food habits of the quail, or bobwhite, has demonstrated beyond question that from an economic point of view it is one of the most valuable of North American birds.—Year Book, U. S. Department of Agriculture, 1903.

The Audubon Societies, who cherish the bird for the pleasure it brings to eye and ear; the sportsman, who loves the whirr of its brown wings bursting from the stubble, and the farmer, whose enemies it destroys and whose resources it enriches, should work together to secure for its preservation laws adequate and generally enforced.—Year Book, U. S. Department of Agriculture, 1903.

This splendid little game bird is not only a seed-eater, but the investigations show that during certain months of the year it is also an insect consumer, the percentage from May to August being over 31 per cent. The gizzards and crops of quail examined in the government laboratories were collected from twenty-one States, besides Canada, District of Columbia and Mexico. Two tablespoonfuls of chinch bugs were found in one quail crop. In one investigation recorded in the year book of the United States Department of Agriculture, 1903, page 196, one hundred and sixteen species of insects were noted as entering into the quail diet.—H. P. Attwater.

To my friend, the quail-shooter and epicure: The next time you regale a good appetite with blue points, terrapin stew, filet of sole and saddle of mutton, touched up here and there with high lights of rare old sherry, rich claret and dry monopole, pause as the dead quail is laid before you, on a funeral pyre of toast, and consider this, "Here lie the charred remains of the farmers' ally and friend, poor bobwhite." In life he devoured

145 different kinds of bad insects, and the seeds of 129 anathema weeds. For the smaller pests of the farm he was the most marvelous engine of destruction that God ever put together of flesh and blood. He was good, beautiful and true; and his small life was blameless. And here he lies, dead; snatched away from his field of labor, and destroyed, in order that I may be tempted to dine three minutes longer, after I have eaten to satisfy."—William F. Hornaday, Campaigning Trustee, Permanent Wild Life and Protection Fund.

Perhaps there is no bird to which the American people are more deeply indebted for both aesthetic and material benefits. He is the most democratic and ubiquitous of all our game birds. He is not a bird of the desert, wilderness, or mountain peak, which one must go far to find. He seeks the home, farm, garden and field; he is the friend and companion of mankind; a much-needed helper on the farm; a destroyer of insect pests and weeds; a swift-flying game bird lying well to the dog; and, last as well as least, good food—a savory morsel, nutritious and digestible.—Edward H. Forbush.

Among some of the useful birds of Texas, perhaps bobwhite ranks among the highest. If the law would place the proper protection around him, he would soon have a home and become a familiar bird on every farm in Texas. The food of this invaluable bird in the course of the year consists largely of potato beetles, the twelve-spotted cucumber beetles, the bean-leaf beetle, the squash ladybird, wire worms and their beetles. May beetles, corn weevils, the imbricated snout beetles, the clover-leaf weevil, the Mexican cotton weevil, the striped garden caterpillar, the army worm, the cotton worm, the bollworm, various species of cutworms, the cornhouse ant, the red-legged grasshopper, and the chinch bug, are all articles of his diet.—S. N. Lesene.

The farmer should regard the quail as one of his most valuable assets. "He is the gleaner who never reaps, who guards the growing crops, who glories over a bounteous yield, yet is content to watch and wait for those lost grains which fall to him by right." These birds are good stubble feeders, gathering in weed seed, waste grain, and insects. They also eat a few wild berries, rose hips, and the like. Included in their diet of animal food are large numbers of ill-tasting insects that are usually rejected by other birds. Among these insects are the potato beetle, the cucumber beetle, and the chinch bug. In a stomach of a single quail has been found 10,000 pigweed seed; in another 1,000 ragweed seeds; in another 5,000 pigeon grass seeds; in another 100 potato beetles, and so on.—The Kansas Industrialist.

One of the most valuable assets of the southern planter is the bobwhite, variously known as quail and partridge. During the summer its food consists almost entirely of insects; and, in the fall and winter, it eats chiefly seeds, many of which are those of weeds noxious to the farmer's interests.

They are very valuable in potato growing districts. A man once pointed out to me a covey of quail that was busy gathering potato bugs. He stated that they had kept his potato field so clear of bugs that he had not found it necessary to use Paris green that season, and he figured that each bird thus saved him at least a dollar in expense.

Being entirely terrestrial in their habits, the birds eat chiefly those insects found on or near the ground. They have thus been proven by our agrcultural experts to be one of the most pronounced natural enemies of the insects injurious to farm and garden crops.

In many districts the killing of quail has progressed to a point where it should be entirely stopped until the birds can recover something of their former numbers—T. Gilbert Pearson.

CIRCULARS, BULLETINS, MAGAZINES AND BOOKS FOR BIRD STUDIES IN SCHOOLS

Requests for all publications listed under the Bureau of Biological Survey and United States Department of Agriculture should be addressed to Joseph A. Arnold, U. S. D. A., Washington, D. C. If they are reported out of print or for sale at a nominal price, write to your Senator or Representative. All members of Congress have a supply of publications at their disposal and it is usually possible to procure this material by writing them for it.

BUREAU BIOLOGICAL SURVEY, WASHINGTON, D. C.

1. Bulletin No. 9—Cuckoos and Shrikes in Their Relation to Agriculture.
2. Bulletin No. 15—Food of the Bobolinks, Blackbirds and Grackles.
3. Bulletin No. 17—Birds of a Maryland Farm.
4. Bulletin No. 21—The Bobwhite and Other Quails of the United States in Their Economic Relations.
5. Bulletin No. 23—The Horned Larks and Their Relation to Agriculture.
6. Bulletin No. 25—Birds That Eat the Cotton Boll Weevil.
7. Bulletin No. 27—The North American Eagles and Their Economic Relations.
8. Bulletin No. 29—The Relation of Birds to the Cotton Boll Weevil.
9. Bulletin No. 44—Food of Our More Important Flycatchers.
10. Bulletin No. 45—Distribution and Migration of North American Herons and Their Allies.
11. Circular No. 61—Hawks and Owls From the Standpoint of the Farmer.
12. Circular No. 64—Destruction of the Cotton Boll Weevil by Birds in Winter.
13. Circular No. 75—Our Vanishing Shore Birds.
14. Year Book, Sept., 1898—Birds as Weed Destroyers.
15. Year Book, Sept., 1913—The American Thrushes Valuable Bird Neighbors.

UNITED STATES DEPARTMENT OF AGRICULTURE, WASHINGTON, D. C.

1. Farmers' Bulletin No. 54—Some Common Birds in Their Relation to Agriculture.
2. Farmers' Bulletin No. 217—Mortality Among Water Fowl Around Great Salt Lake, Utah.
3. Farmers' Bulletin No. 390—Pheasant Raising in the United States.
4. Farmers' Bulletin No. 456—Our Grosbeaks and Their Value to Agriculture.

5. Farmers' Bulletin No. 493—The English Sparrow as a Pest.
6. Farmers' Bulletin No. 506—Food of Some Well-Known Birds of the Forest, Farm and Garden.
7. Farmers' Bulletin No. 513—Fifty Common Birds of the Farm and Garden.
8. Farmers' Bulletin No. 609—Bird Houses and How to Build Them.
9. Farmers' Bulletin No. 630—Some Common Birds Useful to the Farmer.
10. Farmers' Bulletin No. 760—How to Attract Birds in Northwestern United States.
11. Farmers' Bulletin No. 774—Game Laws for 1916.
12. Farmers' Bulletin No. 775—Some Common Birds of Southeastern United States in Relation to Agriculture.
13. Year Book, Sept., 1894—The Crow Blackbirds and Their Food.
14. Year Book, Sept., No. 500—Our Meadow Larks in Relation to Agriculture.
15. Year Book, Sept., No. 642—Our Shorebirds and Their Future.

STATE BOARD OF AGRICULTURE, BOSTON, MASS.

1. No. 48—The Starling.
2. No. 25—Bird Houses and Nesting Boxes.
3. No. 48—The English Sparrow and the Means of Controling It.
4. No. 49—Food Plants to Attract Birds and Protect Fruit.

OTHER HELPFUL MATERIAL

The National Association of Audubon Societies, 1974 Broadway, New York, N. Y.:

1. Attracting Birds About the Home. Price, 10 cents.
2. Educational Leaflets.

Southern Pacific Passenger Department, Houston, Texas:
The Relation of Birds to the Farmer.

The University of Colorado, Boulder, Colorado:
The Practical Value of Birds.

New York State College of Agriculture, Ithaca, N. Y.:
    Birds in Their Relation to Agriculture in New York State.
State Entomologist, St. Anthony Park, Minn.:
    Circular 32, Some Useful Birds Found in Minnesota.
    Circular 35, Further Observations on Minnesota.
    Birds, Their Economic Relations to the Agriculturist.
Kansas Agricultural College, Manhattan, Kansas:
    The Industrialist, Vol. I, No. 5, Bird Life.
Department of College Extension, Agricultural College, North
  Dakota:
    Guide for North Dakota Bird Study.
Wilson Ornithological Club, Chicago, Ill.:
    The Wilson Bulletin, No. 88, Spring Migration at Hous-
      ton, Texas. (1914.)
Texas Department of Agriculture, Austin, Texas:
    Use and Value of Wild Birds.
Department of Extension, University of Texas:
    The Mourning Dove.

Magazines

Bird Lore. D. Appleton & Co., Harrisburg, Pa. $1.50 a year.
The Oologist. R. M. Barnes, Albion, N. Y. 50 cents a year.
The Auk. American Ornithologist Union, Cambridge, Mass.
  $3 a year.
The Condor. Cooper Ornithological Club, Hollywood, Cal. $1.50
  a year.
The Wilson Bulletin. Wilson Ornithological Club, Oberlin,
  Ohio. $1 a year.

BOOKS FOR THE SCHOOL LIBRARY

1. The Bird Study Book. Pearson. $1.25.
2. Stories of Bird Life. Pearson. 60 cents.
3. Bird Guide—Land Birds. Reed. $1.
4. Bird Guide—Water Birds, Game Birds and Birds of Prey.
     Reed. $1.
5. Useful Birds and Their Protection. Forbush. $2.
6. Birds Every Child Should Know. Blanchan. $1.20.

7. Bird Neighbors. Blanchan. $2.
8. Birds That Hunt and Are Hunted. Blanchan. $2.
9. First Book of Birds. Miller. $1.
10. Little Bird Blue. Finley & Finley. 75 cents.
11. What I Have Done With Birds. Porter. $1.25.
12. Birds of the United States East of the Rockies. Chapman. $2.

NOTE.—Books Nos. 1, 3, 4, 6, 7, 8 and 12 may be obtained from Doubleday, Page & Co., Garden City, N. Y. No. 2, from B. F. Johnson Publishing Company, Richmond, Va. No. 5, from State Board of Agriculture, Boston, Mass. Nos. 9, 10 and 11, from Houghton-Mifflin Company, Boston, Mass.

PICTURES AND POST CARDS

1. Miniature Bird Pictures and Nature Post Cards. Chas. L. Reed, Worcester, Mass.
2. The National Association of Audubon Societies.

Every school should have an Audubon Society. The membership fee is ten cents for ten or more. In return for this ten cents each child is presented with eight beautiful colored plates of birds with an outline sheet for a drawing lesson for each, and a nature leaflet telling all about the bird whose picture accompanies it for each of the eight colored plates. Each member also receives a beautiful bird cabinet, containing the colored photographs of sixty-three birds. *Bird Lore*, the splendid magazine of the Societies, is sent free to all schools having an Audubon Club. Write T. Gilbert Pearson, Secretary National Audubon Societies, 1974 Broadway, New York City, for further information.

For further information regarding any suggested material write the Extension Loan Librarian, University of Texas, Austin.

THE CENTURY MAGAZINE.

Vol. XXVI.   AUGUST, 1883.   No. 4.

BOB WHITE, THE GAME BIRD OF AMERICA.

Of all the game birds of America, none is better appreciated by the sportsman than little Bob White. He may be found from southern Maine and Canada to the Gulf, and from the Atlantic to the high central plains, and he is known by various names. In the North and East, he is called Quail; in the South and West, he is Partridge; while everywhere, he is known as Bob White. Let us then call him as he calls himself, and we will not be berated for our ignorance of natural history. In fact, he is neither quail nor partridge; but, to our mind he seems more akin to the latter than to the former of his European cousins. The quail of Europe is a smaller and more dumpy bird than our little friend. His flesh is dark and loaded with fat. His plumage is dull and his aspect plebeian. He does not form into coveys, but flocks at the periods of his migrations, when he flies at night, and in the company of countless numbers, during the month of April crosses the Mediterranean to the European shores and islands, returning to Africa in the autumn.* He is a polygamous, pugnacious, selfish little Arab, and lacks entirely that gallant bearing and affectionate nature which are marked characteristics of the American bird. A wretched husband, he abandons his wives and young to their fate at the waning of the honeymoon; and his selfish manners are inherited by his chicks, who " are hardly full grown when they separate, or, if kept together, fight obstinately, and their quarrels are terminated only by their common destruction." It belies both the appearance and character of Bob White to call him after such a mean-looking, disreputable bird as the European quail.

The common European gray-partridge differs somewhat in form from our bird, which in this particular resembles more closely the red-legged partridge of Europe; but what is said of the habits of Bob White applies equally well to the European partridge. The latter weighs twice as much as Bob White, but he has not Bob's sturdy, rapid, and often long-continued flight. Like our bird, his flesh is white; he forms into coveys; is monogamous, and keeps with his wife and brood till the following spring. He is not migratory or nocturnal in his habits. His wings are similar in form to those of our bird, having the third quill-feather the longest, which is a characteristic of the partridges, and distinguishes them from the quails, which have the first quill-feather the longest.

It is true that Bob White is sometimes partly migratory in his habits. It is said that he has " a running season " in October, when, joining a pack, he leaves the region of his birth and travels on foot in a southerly and easterly direction till he reaches the borders of streams and bays, where he may remain till November, when he returns to his former haunts. During his travels it would be useless to hunt him, for he then runs with great rapidity before the dog and will not take wing.

---

* " The quails assemble at the approach of autumn, to cross the Black Sea over to the southern coast: the order of this emigration is invariable: toward the end of August the quails, in a body, choose one of those fine days when the wind, blowing from the north at sunset, promises them a fine night; they take their departure about seven in the evening, and finish a journey of fifty leagues by break of day,—a wonderful distance for a short-winged bird, and that is generally fat and sluggish of flight."

" Such prodigious quantities have appeared on the western coasts of the kingdom of Naples, in the vicinity of Nettuno, that *one hundred thousand* have in one day been taken, within the space of four or five miles."—*Daniel's "Rural Sports."*

The European partridge and Bob White differ in their call-notes and in their longevity. Daniel, in his superb "Rural Sports," London, 1812, states: "It is said the partridge, if unmolested, lives from fifteen to seventeen years; others dispute this computation, and maintain that they live seven years, and give over laying in the sixth, and are in full vigor when two years old." Dr. Elisha T. Lewis, in his "American Sportsman," Philadelphia, 1857, says that the average duration of Bob White's life is three to five years; but neither of these authors states how these facts were ascertained. Our distinguished ornithologist, Dr. Coues, classes Bob White among the partridges, and says:

"Our partridges [viz. Bob White, the Mountain, Valley, and Massena quails, etc.] may be distinguished among American *Gallinæ*, by the foregoing characters, but not from those of the Old World; and it is highly improbable that, as a group, they are separable from all the forms of the latter by any decided peculiarities. I find that the principal supposed character, namely, a toothing of the under mandible, is very faintly indicated in some forms, and entirely wanting in others. Pending final issue, however, it is expedient to re-organize the group, so strictly limited geographically, if not otherwise. * * * In

If, however, many of our friends should persist—as they certainly will—in calling Bob White a quail, then they should call a brood of these birds *a bevy;* while *a covey* should designate a brood, if they call him a Virginia partridge. The plumage differs so much with latitude, that some naturalists have made out three species: the *Ortyx Virginianus*, the *O. Floridanus*, and the *O. Texanus.* The male of the *Floridanus* is about the size of the female *Virginianus.* Its bill is longer and jet black; its colors are darker and its black markings are heavier. The *Texanus* is of the size of the *Floridanus;* the colors are paler, the prevailing shade being rather gray than brown; upper part much variegated with tawny. Sometimes he dons a coat which is nearly white. One of these little colorless birds is shown in the engraving on page 486. He was shot in the month of November, by Mr. Charles Hallock, near Berlin, in Worcester County, Maryland.

If, after a day of successful shooting over a considerable area, the sportsman will count the number of cock and hen birds which have fallen to his aim, he will find the former al-

"BOB WHITE!"

habits, they agree more or less completely with the well known Bob White: Head completely feathered, and usually crested, the crest frequently assuming a remarkable shape, nasal fosse not filled with feathers; the nostrils covered with a naked scale; tarsi and toes naked, the latter scarcely or not fringed."

ways outnumbering the latter. The **exact** ratio I do not know. I have but once **sepa**rated them; then, in a bag of forty, I found twenty-four cocks to sixteen hens. According to the European naturalist, Ray, the European partridge hatches one-third more males than females.

The average weight of Bob White varies considerably with the nature of his feeding-

of December, that would average eight ounces." Dr. Lewis, in his "American Sportsman," gives a record of ten braces of birds shot in the neighborhood of Mount

PARTRIDGES (PERDIX CINEREA), MALE AND FEMALE.

ground, the weather preceding the time when he is shot, and the age of the bird. Probably six and three-quarter ounces is a fair average weight. In Southern Maryland, I have shot a few cock-birds which weighed eight ounces and one-quarter, and one even as high in weight as eight ounces and three-quarters. Fifty birds shot in the middle of North Carolina, last December, averaged seven ounces. Those birds were cocks and hens, old and young, just as they came to bag in the field. Mr. Frank Schley says: " I have often killed a bag of birds along the Monocacy and Potomac bottoms in Maryland, in the month

Holly, New Jersey, that averaged eight ounces.

While the woodcock and Wilson snipe are fated to disappear as civilization robs them of their restricted feeding-grounds, Bob White, if protected by the enforcement of judicious game laws, will thrive in the midst of cultivated lands, and will continue to test the gamecraft and marksmanship of future generations. He is destined to remain the game-bird of America, and he is worthy of it; for there is none more impetuous in his flight, none that has such extended range in his feeding-grounds and coverts, none that de-

WHITE BOB WHITE.

mands of the gunner more knowledge of his habits in order to find him, and none that tests so well the training of a dog and the eye and nerve of the sportsman. We should be thankful that he, with the black-bass, will be spared in the relentless action of that artificial selection which is slowly but surely taking from us the woodcock, the snipe, the grouse, and the wild trout.

Unlike the grouse and the European quail, our little American is a faithful husband and devoted father. To find Bob in Mormon practices is rare. Should he, however, discover that his gallant bearing and spruce attire have made him doubly beloved, he will show impartial devotion to his two spouses. From a fence-rail overhead, with his two wives on their nests, not two feet apart, he will gladden both their little hearts with his love-song. But he is naturally a monogamist. He selects his mate and makes his courtship in the spring, soon after the snow and frost have gone, when the willows have turned yellow, while the frogs are piping in the marsh, and the Wilson snipe is drumming above the meadows. If the wintry storm should come back, the mates will re-assemble in a covey and keep each other warm o' nights and huddle on the sunny slopes during the day.

In the month of May they build their simple nest, formed of a slight depression in the ground lined with dried leaves and soft grasses. This nest may be found under a tussock of grass, beneath a small bush, in the brier-grown corner of a worm-fence, at the foot of an old stump, alongside a log, or often in the open fields of wheat or clover. The nest is sometimes closed above with stubble mingled with the grass tussock or briers, and provided with a side entrance; but the nest is as often found open above as closed.

In this nest the hen-bird lays from one dozen to two dozen eggs of a pure, brilliant white. While the hen is laying and during her time of nesting, the cock is the happiest of husbands. Filled with joy and pride, he sits on the low bough of a neighboring tree, or perches on the fence-rail quite near his spouse, whom he never wearies of telling that he is "Bob White —your Bob White," in such a brilliant, happy voice that the farmer stops his work to listen to him.

In from three to four weeks the little downy young leave the egg, and even with pieces

BOB WHITE AND EUROPEAN QUAIL. (COTURNIX COMMUNIS.)

of egg-shell yet sticking on their backs they go off with their parents to be taught to search for food. They feed on the seeds of various grasses, weeds, and cereals, and on berries; and they return a hundred-fold the bounty of their landlord, by destroying for his benefit not only countless numbers of destructive insects, but quantities of weed-seed, one to two gills of which the adult birds can stow away in their little crops during a day's feeding.

If rain should come on, or the cold wind blow, the mother calls her younglings under her wings, where they nestle safe from the chilling storm.

BOB WHITE EGG (FULL SIZE).

When night comes on, she and her spouse take their little ones to some place removed from the thicket, where prowl the fox and the weasel. Soon after being hatched, the young, in running, assist themselves with their tiny wings, and when two weeks old they take wing with a flutter that is very amusing to those familiar with the startling whir of the old birds. When too large to gather under the mother they take their flight at night-fall, from the stubble or grain field where they have been feeding, and thus, breaking the scent, drop down in a compact cloud into some open space under a bush or tussock, and cozily huddling up to one another, form a little circle with their heads outward. Thus nestled, they see on all sides, and can spring at a moment from their bed to evade any foe that may steal on them in the night or at the early dawn. If the ground be covered with snow or hoar frost, or the weather be wet or blustering, they may remain huddled together all day, or may not venture to feed till late in the forenoon. But if they are greeted with the sunrise and good weather, they cheep a good-morning to one another in soft, cheerful voices, and go at once to their feeding-grounds, where they regale themselves on the wheat of the stubbles, the buckwheat, the seeds of grasses, and the rag-weed, and on the berries of the haw, the gum, and the chicken-grape. About ten or eleven o'clock they retire to the sunny side of a covert, and they do not venture forth again till three or four in the afternoon, when they again seek their food till sundown and bed-time.

In October and November, the sportsman often "springs" coveys containing birds too small to be shot; sometimes half the covey will be in this condition, the other half full-grown birds. This fact may be accounted for thus: The eggs and the young are often destroyed by the wet and cold of the early summer, or by beasts and birds of prey. If this calamity should overtake them, the hen again goes to laying, and this second brood is retarded by the time lost between the first and second nestings. When birds of two sizes are found in the same covey, it seems to show that the parents have raised two broods; and this, I think, happens oftener to the south than to the north of the James River,—the summer of our middle and and northern States being generally too short for the raising of two broods. Baird says: "They have two broods in a season, the second in August"; while Audubon states that "in Texas, the Floridas, and as far eastward as the neighborhood of Charleston, in South Carolina, it breeds twice in the year, first in May, and again in September."

AT DAWN.

The cock-bird shares with the hen the duties and restraints of incubation. If his spouse should desire another brood, he will take charge of the half-grown young while she makes her second nesting. When the second brood appears, it runs with the first, and they form together one happy family, and remain with their parents till the following spring, in the pairing season, when the old family ties are severed.

The devotion of the parents to their unfledged young, and the real affection which the members of a family have for one another up to the time of their separation in the spring, have been so touchingly described by two of the most gifted of our writers on field sports, that I must here quote them; especially as the writings of W. P. Hawes ("J. Cypress, Jr.") are now rarely met with. He says:

"If you would see the purest, the sincerest, the most affecting piety of a parent's love, startle a family of young quails and watch the conduct of the mother. She will not leave you. No, not she. But she will fall at your feet, uttering a noise which none but a distressed mother can make, and she will run, and flutter, and seem to try to be caught, and cheat your outstretched hand, and affect to be wing-broken, and wounded, and yet have just strength to tumble along, until she has drawn you, fatigued, a safe distance from her threatened children, and the hopes of her young heart; and then she will mount, whirring with glad strength, and away through the maze of trees you had not seen before, like a close-shot bullet, fly to her skulking infants. Listen, now! Do you hear those three half-plaintive notes, quickly and clearly poured out? She is calling the boys and girls together. She sings not now 'Bob White!' nor 'Ah! Bob White!' That is her husband's love-call, or his trumpet-blast of defiance. But she calls sweetly and softly for her lost children. Hear them 'Peep! peep! peep!' at the welcome voice of their mother's love! They are coming together. Soon the whole family will meet again."

The following is by Henry William Herbert ("Frank Forrester"):

"Unlike the young broods of the woodcock, which are mute, save the twitter with which they rise, the bevies of quail appear to be attached to each other by tender affection. If dispersed by accidental causes, either in the pursuit of their food, or from being flushed by some casual intruder, so soon as their first alarm has passed over, they begin calling to each other with a small, plaintive note, quite different from the amorous whistle of the male bird, and from their merry, day-break cheeping, and each one running toward the sound, and repeating it at intervals, they soon collect themselves together into one happy little family.

"If, however, the ruthless sportsman has been

CALIFORNIA VALLEY PARTRIDGE OR QUAIL.   (LOPHORTYX CALIFORNICUS.)

among them with his well-trained setter and unerring gun, so that death has sorely thinned their numbers, they will protract their little call for their lost comrades even to night-fall; and in such cases — I know not if it be fancy on my part — there has often seemed to me to be an unusual degree of melancholy in their wailing whistle.

"Once this struck me especially. I had found a small bevy of thirteen birds in an orchard, close to the house in which I was passing a portion of the autumn, and in a very few minutes killed twelve of them, for they lay hard in the tedded clover, and it was perfectly open shooting. The thirteenth and last bird, rising with two others which I killed right and left, flew but a short distance and dropped among some sumacs in the corner of a rail fence. I could have shot him certainly enough, but some undefined feeling induced me to call my dog to heel, and spare his little life; yet afterward I almost regretted what I certainly intended at the time for mercy. For day after day, so long as I remained in the country, I heard his sad call from morn till dewy eve, crying for his departed friends, and full, apparently, of memory, which is, alas! but too often another name for sorrow.

"It is a singular proof how strong is the passion for the chase and the love of pursuit implanted by nature in the heart of man, that however much, when not influenced by the direct heat of sport, we depre-

cate the killing of these little birds, and pity the individual sufferers, the moment the dog points and the bevy springs, or the propitious morning promises good sport, all the compunction is forgotten in the eagerness and emulation which are natural to our race."

Bob White schools the wing-shot as severely as the wily trout tries the angler. Like the trout, he has habits which we must be acquainted with in order to find him. If the weather be fair, start early, for the birds will be on their feeding-grounds at sunrise, and will be found in the fields of stubble, or in the midst of the rag-weed, and along the brier-fringed ditches; and do not forget the field of buckwheat, for they are especially fond of it. About ten or eleven they will cease feeding, and will seek the sunny side of some covert near a stream, where they will quench their thirst after their morning meal. Here they will dust and preen themselves, and take their noonday siesta. The birds will generally remain here till three or four hours after mid-

EUROPEAN RED-LEGGED PARTRIDGE. (CACCABIS RUFA.)

drop your aim just *under* him while he is only momentarily in sight.

If you had a fair day yesterday, but after a long spell of wet weather, and you returned home last night in a clear, cold, quiet air, you may expect to see the sunshine of to-morrow sparkling in the hoar frost which covers the ground and all the herbage. Tarry at home till the sun has nearly melted the ice off the meadows, for you will get nothing but wet legs by tramping the fields while the ground is iced and while the birds are yet huddled and have not spread their scent.

When the dogs are seeking the coveys, let them range widely. When they stand the covey, do not exhaust yourself with haste in reaching them, but approach leisurely and quietly. When the covey springs be very quick, but very, *very* steady, and do not fire till you are sure of your aim. Remember that it is your left arm and wrist that direct your gun; so grasp it well forward on the fore-end, and not near the breech, as some do. You will thus be able to give your gun that quick and firm motion which is indispensable to skill in " snap-shooting "; and all shooting at Bob White is of that character.

If it is your first shot of the season, and you are not gifted with a very steady nerve, you will do well to charge your gun with but one cartridge. By doing so, it is probable that a bird will drop to your first shot. If you had had two shots, you might have been too anxious for two birds, and thus have lost both. After two or three successes with a single barrel, try " a double " over the next point.

Always flush the birds yourself, for a dog " hied on " to flush may do so of his own accord when you are out of gunshot. At the springing of the covey, the dog must " down charge," or " drop to shot," and in either case hold his charge till ordered to "hold up" or to " seek dead." If he " break shot," he will often cause you great vexation in the loss of shots by his flushing birds which did not spring with their fellows, but which now get up in rapid succession, and before you have had time to reload. But a good retriever has his greatest pleasure in fetching a dead bird, and the intense satisfaction this act gives to him often causes him to lose his head and rush in on the report of the gun. The dropping to shot and retaining charge is one of

day, and closely huddled as they are. they are difficult for the dog to find.

The sportsman, if wise, will now follow the example of the birds, and seeking the quiet of some sheltered sunny nook, will take his lunch and rest himself and his dogs. How well we remember that pleasant spring side, with the dogs stretched before us to catch the warm rays of the sun, their eyes furtively glancing at us, waiting for their share of the lunch ; the fragrant cigar, with pleasant jokes at our bad shots and untimely tumble, the generous admiration of our companions' skill, and talk about the wonderful working of the dogs.

If the weather is very dry, do not seek the birds on the uplands, for Bob White, though no hydropathist, likes the vicinity of water. But if your hunt occurs after a rainy spell, go to the upland stubble-fields, and work your dogs along the border of the driest and sunniest of the coverts.

If it is windy and cold, the birds will be found in covert along the sunny lee slopes of the valleys, in the tall rag-weed and briers of the hollows, and on the sunny borders of the woods and hedge-rows. They will not now lie well to the dog, and when flushed will go like bullets into the deepest thickets. Should you hope to prevent this by getting them in between you and the dogs, you may often be mistaken, for in all likelihood they will spring over your head like sparks from under a blacksmith's hammer. The shooting is now difficult, for you will have to turn rapidly on your heel as the bird passes over you, and

MRS. BOB WHITE AND FAMILY.

the prime requisites in a dog, and is as difficult to teach a good retriever as it is essential
to the true enjoyment of sport.

If the dog is unsteady and apt to "break
shot," do not load if you have fired only
one barrel, for in so doing other birds may
rise just as you have opened your gun or
are handling a cartridge.

After the covey has been scattered give
your dog but little range. Keep your eye
well on him as you approach the ground
where you or your gillie has marked the birds.
Be ready, if he be rash when he "winds" the
birds, to chide him, in a voice just sufficient
to be heard. *Steady, there! Toho!*

Above all things, do not get excited and
gain in voice as you lose in temper. Take it
leisurely, be quiet and cool, if you would enjoy the sport and kill cleanly. By all means,
train your dog, if possible, to hunt without
shouting to him. A short, quick whistle should
call his attention. Then give him the order
he waits for by waves of the hand : forward,
for "on"; a wave to the right or left, as you
may desire him to quarter; while the upraised
arm, with the palm of your hand toward him,
should bring him to "toho." Or, two short
whistles may be often better for the same

order, while one much prolonged should
bring him "to heel."

A dog that with head well up winds his
birds and is stanch on a covey, that will
drop to shot and retain his charge till ordered
to retrieve, and will receive and obey your
orders from the whistle and the motions of
your arm and hand, is a dog indeed. Such
dogs exist. Should you shoot over such a one,
make a note of him as having the education
which your next puppy shall receive. You may
never possess such a dog; but if a true sportsman, you will ever endeavor to have one like
him.

After the covey has been flushed and shot
at and the birds have been well scattered, the
real enjoyment in Bob White shooting begins.
One may now have single and double shots
over all kinds of ground and at birds taking
every conceivable direction of flight. But
often, the best of markers will be baffled in
finding the birds whose flight he has carefully
noted after the springing of the covey. The
following incident is typical of the experience
of all sportsmen : A large covey was once
flushed and shot at, three birds falling to our
fire. My friend and I watched the other birds
as they flew across a swale, where we sprung

them, and we saw them sail with extended wings over a large field on the valley slope, into which they dropped after a few flutters of their wings. There could be no doubt as to the whereabouts of the birds, because the whole field, from its inclination to our line of sight, was in full view, and was quite an open sedge field with its surface sparsely studded with stunted pines. On our approach to the field, the dogs quartered it, but they did not come to a stand. One dog flushed a bird on which he came suddenly, and he at once "charged." We found the dogs useless, and calling them to " heel," we walked slowly into the sedge. When we were about in the center of the field, the birds began to rise successively and singly in all directions; in front, on our side, and sometimes behind us, giving us delightful shots. Similar experiences recurring so often have made some sportsmen suppose that Bob White has a voluntary power of retaining his scent, and thus in time of danger eludes the dogs. But this well known occurrence can be explained otherwise. Often when the frightened birds alight, they do not run but instantly crouch with their wings closely pressed against their bodies, so as to squeeze themselves into the smallest compass. This act, no doubt, causes a diminution in the emission of their effluvia. But if the birds have run after alighting, the dogs will surely find them, provided they do not run rapidly and to great distances; in which case the dogs are baffled by the multiplicity of scents; and especially will this be so if the dog gets on the trail of a bird which doubles like a hare on its track.

This baffling of a dog on ground containing a recently scattered covey shows that time should be allowed for the birds to recover from their confusion and to begin to run together, before you " hie on " the dogs to find them. If you are familiar with the country and can remember the landmarks, the proper method is to flush two or three coveys, and then begin to hunt the scattered birds of the respective coveys in the order in which you flushed them.

To become a successful shot at Bob White, the sportsman should bear in mind that Bob, immediately after he has sprung, flies with a velocity which probably exceeds that of any other bird; and also that, unless fairly hit, he can carry off a large number of pellets. When a covey springs, it rises at a considerable angle with the ground. Hence, in shooting at a bird in a flushed covey, the sportsman of unsteady nerve and sluggish muscles is apt to undershoot, the bird rising with such velocity that by the time the gunner has brought his gun into position the bird has passed above his line of sight. As a rule, I think that about one second generally elapses between the instant of springing of the bird and the moment of fire. This interval gives the bird time to gain a moderately horizontal line of flight, and allows the sportsman to get a fair aim.

In shooting at an incoming bird, let him be out of sight and just below the rib of your gun at the moment of firing. At a bird going overhead, wait till he has passed well over; then shoot under him. At straightaway shots hold a little high, so that you just catch a glimpse of the bird over your barrels.

In shooting at cross shots, it should be understood that the velocity of an ounce of No. 8 shot driven with three drams of powder is near to 900 feet per second. In that second a Bob White, if under full headway, will go 88 feet, if we estimate the velocity of his flight so low as only a mile a minute. If he is flying directly across your line of sight and thirty yards off, the shot will take one-tenth of a second to reach that distance, and in one-tenth of a second the bird has gone over eight and eight-tenths feet. So, if we should fire a snap-shot directly at a cross-flying bird thirty yards distant, the center of the cloud of shot would fall about nine feet behind him, and he would pass by unscathed. To kill him " clean," you must hold nine feet ahead of him. To some sportsmen, nine feet may seem a great distance to " hold ahead " on a cross-flying bird thirty yards away, but not to those who have noticed attentively the relations of the line of their aim to the position of the bird *at the very moment they hear the report of their gun.* Also, estimations of distances in the air beside a small and quickly moving object are very unreliable, and often when the sportsman thinks he has fired only one foot ahead of a bird he has really held ahead three feet. Let some one suspend horizontally in the air an unfamiliar object that must be distant from fence rails and other things whose dimensions you know, and then guess its length. You will, after a few trials, be satisfied that the estimation of actual lengths at thirty yards is very loose guess-work.

Bob White is a tough and hardy little fellow, and the true sportsman, always a humane man, will remember this and endeavor to kill him outright. This can be done only by hitting him fairly with the center of the charge. Often a bird will fly two or three hundred yards though mortally wounded. It is the duty of all sportsmen to watch carefully the flight of the birds he has shot at, and his experience of the nature of their flight will tell him if the bird has been struck. If he concludes that he has been, then it is his bounden duty to bring that bird to bag, and that right quickly.

The extraordinary vitality of this vigorous bird was once forcibly impressed on me. A covey was flushed at about one hundred yards from the edge of a wood. Only a few of the birds flew to the woods. One of them, going at a tremendous velocity, crossed my position at a distance of about forty yards. Holding my gun at what I judged was the proper distance ahead of him, I fired. This was the only shot fired at the birds making for the wood.

"Sam," said I to our negro gillie, "I think I hit that bird."

"No, sah," said Sam; "I tink not, sah. He's a-gwine to whah he forgit he lef' suf-fin, sah!"

Sam is a good marker, and has carefully watched the flight of hundreds of birds shot at. Yet I could not entirely satisfy myself that the bird was not fairly hit, though he kept straight on in his vigorous flight. A sprained foot prevented rapid walking, and my companion entered the wood, with the dogs, before me. As I struck the edge of the woods I heard the report of his gun, and after proceeding about one hundred yards I heard a second shot, and in another instant a bird tumbled through the air and fell about a dozen feet in advance of me. I called out:

"I have them both!"

"Both what?" said he. "I only shot one bird, and the other flew away from your direction and I missed him clean."

The bird my friend shot lay with his head toward me; the other, a large cock, lay on his back with his bill pointing toward the other bird, and not more than a foot from him. Both birds were warm. The large cock was the one I had fired at. He was struck fairly in the head and chest, and yet he had pitched into the woods and gone altogether nearly two hundred yards before he succumbed to his death-wounds. But for the remarkable circumstances which led to the finding of this bird, I should never have surely known that I had shot him.

Rules for shooting are of value, and directions founded on theory may serve to inform the beginner why he misses and thus show him the way to improvement in his marksmanship; but no matter how well we may know *how* the shooting should be done, *to do it* is an art which can be attained only by the assiduous cultivation and development of certain peculiar natural gifts.

A beginner who, out of three shots can bring one Bob White to bag, need not be discouraged or ashamed; with sufficient practice, he may one day kill one out of two birds fired at. The sportsman who does not select his shots (and no man really a sportsman *can* do that), but takes his chances in the open and in covert on all birds which offer a probability of success to his skill, and who, the season through, brings to his bag three out of five birds fired at, is an accomplished sportsman. If he can make three successful shots out of four, he is a phenomenal marksman.

Last season, I shot with the best wing-shot I ever hunted with. At my request, this gentleman, Mr. H. K. B. Davis, of Philadelphia, has written for me the following statement; which, coming from one who has had such unusual opportunities in hunting Bob White, in North Carolina, cannot fail to be of interest to all sportsmen:

"I find, on referring to my record containing the number of coveys found and the number of birds killed, that the average is but little over three birds brought to bag from each covey flushed. When it is remembered that the usual number of birds found in a covey runs from ten to eighteen, it will give some idea of the difficulties to be overcome, and the large proportion of birds that escape even with good shooting, as the same record shows that seventy-three out of every hundred birds shot at were brought to bag. This record, extending over four years and running up into the thousands of birds killed, gives very reliable data to base calculations upon.

"The dogs I hunted with I have every reason to believe are above the average in speed, endurance, and scenting powers; so there is only one conclusion to arrive at, and that is that these birds are exceedingly difficult both to find and to kill.

"There are many opinions as to the proper method of shooting on the wing. Some hold that 'snap-shooting' is the only way to shoot successfully. Snap-shooting is generally understood to consist in putting the gun to the shoulder and firing the instant it is in position; making the allowance to the right, left, under, or above, as the case may require, before raising the gun; just as you point your finger, instinctively, to any object without having to sight along it. Others are just as sure that no one ever shot decently unless he followed the bird with the sight on the gun and covered it before firing. Some, again, insist that you must swing your gun along with the course of the bird after pulling the trigger. In my opinion, every one who has shot very much acquires a style peculiar to himself, and depending on his temperament and the kinds of birds he has had the most practice on.

"It may be well to give a few hints as to the necessary allowance to be made in taking aim at a bird flying so rapidly as Bob White. The most difficult shot is a bird coming directly toward you, and flying about twenty feet above the ground. I have been quite successful in this shot, by holding directly at the bird until he is within range, and then, just as I touch the trigger, I raise the muzzle of the gun about six inches. I would only advise trying this shot where there is more than one bird, and you want to use the second barrel. When there is only one incoming bird, wait until he passes over you, and then by shooting under him, more or less, according to the speed and elevation at which he is flying, you will be pretty sure to kill.

"In cross shots, at thirty yards and over, hold above the line of flight and from six to nine feet ahead of the bird. This may seem entirely too much, but I have frequently shot Bob White when flying parallel to a rail-fence, when I aimed the full length of the rail ahead of him, this being nearly twelve feet."

The shooting of Bob White demands such quick action in handling the gun, and such long tramps to discover his retreats, that I would advise light guns for his pursuit. A pound more in weight will be felt in the afternoon of a long day's hunt, and the rapidity and ease with which a light and short gun can be handled, makes it very efficient in snap-shooting in covert. A twelve-gauge seven-pound gun, of twenty-eight-inch barrels, carrying one ounce of No. 8 shot and three drams of powder, or a sixteen-gauge of six pounds weight and twenty-six-inch barrels, charged with seventh-eighths of an ounce of shot and two and three-quarter drams of powder, is to my liking in this most enjoyable of field sports; in which occupation may next season find you, my sportsman reader, when,

"Full of the expected sport, your heart beats high
As, with impatient steps, you haste to reach
The stubbles where the scattered grain affords
A sweet repast to the yet heedless game.
Near yonder hedge-row where high grass and ferns
The secret hollow shade, your pointers stand.
How beautiful they look! With outstretched tails,
With heads immovable and eyes fast fixed,
One fore-leg raised and bent, the other firm,
Advanced forward, presses on the ground."

Alfred M. Mayer.